Smoke and Mirrors

by

Joseph Goodrich

New York Hollywood London Toronto

SAMUELFRENCH.COM

Cover design by Eileen Connolly

Copyright © 2008 by Joseph Goodrich

ALL RIGHTS RESERVED

CAUTION: Professionals and amateurs are hereby warned that *SMOKE AND MIRRORS* is subject to a royalty. It is fully protected under the copyright laws of the United States of America, the British Commonwealth, including Canada, and all other countries of the Copyright Union. All rights, including professional, amateur, motion picture, recitation, lecturing, public reading, radio broadcasting, television and the rights of translation into foreign languages are strictly reserved. In its present form the play is dedicated to the reading public only.

The amateur live stage performance rights to *SMOKE AND MIRRORS* are controlled exclusively by Samuel French, Inc., and royalty arrangements and licenses must be secured well in advance of presentation. PLEASE NOTE that amateur royalty fees are set upon application in accordance with your producing circumstances. When applying for a royalty quotation and license please give us the number of performances intended, dates of production, your seating capacity and admission fee. Royalties are payable one week before the opening performance of the play to Samuel French, Inc., at 45 W. 25th Street, New York, NY 10010.

Royalty of the required amount must be paid whether the play is presented for charity or gain and whether or not admission is charged.

Stock royalty quoted upon application to Samuel French, Inc.

For all other rights than those stipulated above, apply to: The William Morris Agency, LLC, 1325 Avenue of the Americas, New York, NY 10019 Attn: Jonathan Lomma.

Particular emphasis is laid on the question of amateur or professional readings, permission and terms for which must be secured in writing from Samuel French, Inc.

Copying from this book in whole or in part is strictly forbidden by law, and the right of performance is not transferable.

Whenever the play is produced the following notice must appear on all programs, printing and advertising for the play: "Produced by special arrangement with Samuel French, Inc."

Due authorship credit must be given on all programs, printing and advertising for the play.

ISBN 978-0-573-66278-2   Printed in U.S.A.   #20721

No one shall commit or authorize any act or omission by which the copyright of, or the right to copyright, this play may be impaired.

No one shall make any changes in this play for the purpose of production.

Publication of this play does not imply availability for performance. Both amateurs and professionals considering a production are strongly advised in their own interests to apply to Samuel French, Inc., for written permission before starting rehearsals, advertising, or booking a theatre.

No part of this book may be reproduced, stored in a retrieval system, or transmitted in any form, by any means, now known or yet to be invented, including mechanical, electronic, photocopying, recording, videotaping, or otherwise, without the prior written permission of the publisher.

IMPORTANT BILLING AND CREDIT REQUIREMENTS

All producers of *SMOKE AND MIRRORS* must give credit to the Author of the Play in all programs distributed in connection with performances of the Play, and in all instances in which the title of the Play appears for the purposes of advertising, publicizing or otherwise exploiting the Play and/or a production. The name of the Author *must* appear on a separate line on which no other name appears, immediately following the title and *must* appear in size of type not less than fifty percent of the size of the title type.

"Originally Produced by The Flea Theater, New York City 2007"

CHARACTERS

MOSES
ANITA
TERRY
TAMMIE
CHAD
DREW
ESTELLE

All wear some combination of navy-blue and black.

All wear – clipped to a pocket or dangling from a chain around the neck – a photo-I.D. badge.

AUTHOR'S NOTE

Some states have banned 'real' cigarettes on stage. If you live in one of those states, or if actual cigarettes pose a problem to the actors or to the audience, herbal cigarettes should be used.

It is permissible for the number of cigarettes smoked during a performance to vary from what's indicated in the script.

(A large, self-contained room.

Side and back walls are a translucent milky-white.

Front wall – the wall facing the audience – is clear glass or plastic.

Regular door and emergency exit.

Plain black-plastic chairs.

Plain black-plastic tables, each with a plain black-plastic ashtray.

Plain black-plastic trashbin.

A poster in a black-plastic frame – a reproduction of a Monet or a Cezanne painting – and a large digital clock with red numbers provide the only color and decoration in the room.

The room is miked. Dialogue is heard through unseen amplifiers.

1.

(Clock: 6:42.

Darkness.

Dim light up in room.

MOSES – *black suit and tie, sky-blue shirt, black oxfords – enters.*

He flips a switch on the wall.

Harsh light.

He unclips a small walkie-talkie from his waistband.)

MOSES. Tammie. I'm here in Coffin Nail. All clear…Unlock the front doors, please…I'll be back in about ten minutes. I'm gonna check the restrooms and maybe stroll through Transportation…You're an angel. I kiss you all over.

(He exits.

Silence.

ANITA – *with a cup of coffee – enters. She sits, lights a cigarette.*

Silence.

TERRY – *with a cup of coffee and a newspaper – enters. He sits, lights a cigarette, opens his newspaper, reads.*

Silence.)

ANITA. How's it goin'? *(Pause.)*
TERRY. It's goin'.

(Silence.)

How you? *(Pause.)*

ANITA. My sister's in jail – in Chicago – for murder. *(Pause.)*
TERRY. That's fucked up. *(Pause.)* That's fucked up. *(Pause.)* That's fucked up.
ANITA. I know it's fucked up.
TERRY. What she do?

ANITA. Killed her boyfriend. He was beating on her, and she killed him. *(Pause.)* Our dad went to the hospital and she's beat up pretty bad. *(Pause.)* I can't believe it – she killed the guy.

(Silence.)

TERRY. Think that's bad – my brother just got convicted as a habitual.

ANITA. For what?

TERRY. This time? Burglary. *(Pause.)*

ANITA. How old is he?

TERRY. 52.

ANITA. He's gonna be in jail the rest of his life.

TERRY. He *been* in jail all his life. Hell, he been in jail all *my* life. *(Pause.)* Last time I seen him's the last time he was outta jail. *(Pause.)* He was up for habitual then. Spent two years in the workhouse fightin' it. *(Pause.)* It's fucked up.

ANITA. Hell yes.

TERRY. It's fucked up. *(Pause.)*

ANITA. The things people do…

(Silence.)

How was your weekend?

TERRY. Good.

(Silence.)

How's yours?

ANITA. Good. Didn't do anything, but at least I wasn't here, right?

(Silence.)

I ran into Jason on Saturday.

TERRY. No shit? What's he up to?

ANITA. He's got a new girlfriend.

TERRY. How old?

ANITA. 14. 15. Hard to tell. I saw him at the mall. Looked like he had about half of South High with him.

(Pause.)

TERRY. He fuckin' her?

ANITA. I guess. I didn't ask, you know? *(Pause.)* Fat nasty freak. Why can't he get a girl his own age?

TERRY. No one his own age'd fuck him, he so big.

ANITA. That's the truth. *(Pause.)*

TERRY. How big is she? The little schoolgirl?

ANITA. She's a toothpick. You know Marcia?

TERRY. Yeah.

ANITA. She's shorter than Marcia and about ten pounds lighter. *(Pause.)*

TERRY. Man, that'd be like watchin' a toothpick fuckin' a donut, know what I'm sayin'?

ANITA. I don't even wanna think about it.

TERRY. Too late.

(Silence.)

ANITA. They're gonna throw that freak in jail someday.

TERRY. Hell, they'll throw his ass *under* the jail. You know? *Under* the Goddamn jail.

ANITA. He's gonna end up in jail, too.

TERRY. You know it. *(Pause.)*

ANITA. Fat nasty ugly freak.

(Silence.

*(***TAMMIE** *– black suit and tie, sky-blue shirt, black oxfords, cup of coffee in hand – enters.*

She sits, lights a cigarette.)

TAMMIE. Hi.

ANITA. Hello.

TAMMIE. Hi.

TERRY. Hey.

(Silence.)

TAMMIE. Is that today's paper?

TERRY. Uh-huh.

TAMMIE. Can I look at the horoscope?

*(***TERRY** *holds out a section of the paper.*

TAMMIE *takes it, reads.)*

ANITA. Moses give you a break?

TAMMIE. …Yeah. *(Pause.)*

ANITA. Is it good?

TAMMIE. It's okay. It's okay.

ANITA. Would you read mine? Please?…Gemini. *(Pause.)*

TAMMIE. 'Don't be provoked by what is going on around you.'

ANITA. Whooh.

TAMMIE. 'A superior would like nothing better than to rattle you.'

ANITA. Diane. I knew it.

TAMMIE. 'Don't be rattled. Do your job and remain calm, and you will survive the storm. Tonight: Tend to household duties – then relax. You've earned it.'

ANITA. …Wow.

*(***TAMMIE** *re-folds the section of newspaper, returns it to* **TERRY***.*

She sits.)

I guess I better stay calm then.

TERRY. Havin' trouble with Diane?

ANITA. Who isn't?

TERRY. Diane with the hat or Diane the boss?

ANITA. Diane the boss.

TERRY. Oh, she's a pig.

ANITA. A pig in stretch pants.

(Silence.)

TAMMIE. Either of you know anything about pet insurance? *(Pause.)*

TERRY. Little bit, yeah.

TAMMIE. I had to put my cat to sleep on Saturday. They should pay for that, right?

TERRY. That's why you got the insurance.

TAMMIE. That's what I thought. It wasn't like I wasn't gonna pay it, but I should get something from the policy, right? They should cover that, right?

TERRY. Right. *(Pause.)*

TAMMIE. I was looking at the policy – afterwards – and I guess I coulda kept him alive for another six months, but...

TERRY. Yeah, but with all the chemo and shit, he wouldn'ta been happy. *(Pause.)*

ANITA. Your cat died?

TAMMIE. Yeah.

(Silence.)

ANITA. I don't know what I'd do if something happened to Snick...

(She takes a small photograph out of her purse, gives it to **TAMMIE.** *)*

That's Snick.

TAMMIE. ...Oh, for cute!

(She gives the photo back to **ANITA.**

ANITA *crosses to* **TERRY.** *)*

ANITA. You wanna see my dog?

(She gives the photo to **TERRY.** *)*

TERRY. ...Huh. Little clown suit, huh?

ANITA. That was at a birthday party.

(She crosses back to her table, puts the photo away. Silence.)

TAMMIE. What'd you say his name was?

ANITA. Her name.

TAMMIE. Sorry.

ANITA. Her name's Snick. Short for Sunshine Snicklefritz.

TAMMIE. That's so cute.

ANITA. I don't know what I'd do without her. I really don't.

(Silence.)

TERRY. …Huh. They found that little girl. *(Pause.)*

TAMMIE. Which one?

TERRY. The one from Hastings. *(Pause.)*

ANITA. She okay?

TERRY. Chopped her head off.

(Silence.)

TAMMIE. Anyone know what's for lunch today? *(Pause.)*

TERRY. They wrote it on that thing.

TAMMIE. What thing?

TERRY. Thing on the wall.

TAMMIE. What'd it say?

TERRY. Didn't read it. *(Pause.)*

ANITA. I think it's a Tex-Mex kinda thing.

TAMMIE. That means they'll have those good chips. With that stuff. That sauce.

ANITA. Salsa?

TAMMIE. Yeah. *(Pause.)*

ANITA. I like salsa.

TAMMIE. It's good. *(Pause.)* Spicy. *(Pause.)* I like it.

ANITA. Some people don't.

TAMMIE. That salsa's good. *(Pause.)* If it's the same stuff as last time.

(Silence.)

ANITA. Guacamole's good, too. But they never have it.

TAMMIE. I noticed that.

(Silence.)

ANITA. Muffin-Pan Crispies for dessert.

TAMMIE. What?

ANITA. Muffin-Pan Crispies.

(Silence.)

TAMMIE. Anything like Rice Krispy Bars?

ANITA. No, they're more like…muffins. A small muffin. Sort of. You make 'em in a muffin-pan. There's cinnamon and nutmeg and rolled-oats and brown sugar and vanilla extract, and it's sort of a small muffin-cookie-like thing with a crispy glaze…

(Silence.)

I was talking to the food-service guy.

(Silence.)

TAMMIE. I'll try 'em.

(Silence.)

TERRY. I like those shortbread cookies outta the machine myself.

(Silence.)

TAMMIE. Well…

(She stands.)

ANITA. Guess it's that time…

*(**ANITA** stands.*

They move toward the door.)

… Sorry about your cat.

TAMMIE. Thanks.

(They exit.

***TERRY** reads.*

Lights fade.)

2.

(Clock: 10:16.

ESTELLE, *alone, smokes and pages through a notebook.*

Silence.)

CHAD *(Off)* So the weird thing about it all is that she was right. She –

*(***CHAD*** and ***DREW*** *– both in blood-spattered lab coats over dark suits, each with a cup of coffee – enter.)*

DREW. Hey, Estelle.

CHAD. How ya doin'?

*(***ESTELLE*** *grinds out her cigarette, rises.*

CHAD *and ***DREW*** *sit.*

ESTELLE *put her notebook in her purse, and exits.*

CHAD *and ***DREW*** *light cigarettes.*

CHAD *sniffs his sleeve.)*

CHAD. Is it that bad?

DREW. I don't know. I can't tell anymore. *(Pause.)*

CHAD. Does anyone know exactly what she does around here?

DREW. I think she used to be in Administration. *(Pause.)*

CHAD. Huh. *(Pause.)* Anyway – the weird thing about the whole thing was is that everything she said came true. Six years later – to the day – the woman I was with at the time gave birth to a child.

DREW. Was it a girl, though?

CHAD. It was a girl. Six years to the day of that party. I called the fortune teller up and told her. Said she wasn't surprised…Oh – I forgot to mention this part: She said the mother of my child would be a woman named Maria.

DREW. And?

CHAD. The name of the mother of my child…is Maria.

(Silence.

DREW *picks up a section of the paper.)*

DREW. ...I heard about this guy on the news. *(Pause.)* Found him in a ditch somewhere. So dehydrated it was like he'd lost the equivalent of six quarts of water.

CHAD. Fuck.

DREW. Broken leg, too. From the accident. *(Pause.)*

CHAD. Car wreck?

DREW. Motorcycle.

(Silence.)

CHAD. Wearin' a helmet?

DREW. ...No.

CHAD. Always wear a helmet when you're ridin' a motorcycle. That way you can have an open casket. *(Pause.)*

(They laugh.

Silence.)

DREW. I made a very important decision once based on what a fortune teller told me.

CHAD. What was it?

DREW. Now, it turned out she was wrong – or I was wrong, I'm not sure which – but by that point it was too late... Anyway, it all turned out in the end. *(Pause.)*

CHAD. What'd she tell you?

DREW. Told me not to do it. *(Pause.)* But I did it, anyway.

(MOSES enters.)

CHAD. Moses. What's up?

MOSES. Am I interrupting anything?

DREW. You married, Moses?

MOSES. ...Not any more, no.

DREW. Divorced?

MOSES. My wife was murdered.

CHAD. Wow. Sorry.

MOSES. It's all right. I'm over it. Listen – sometime this afternoon, may I have a word with you guys?

DREW. What about?
MOSES. Would sometime after lunch be okay?
CHAD. Is that all right with you?
DREW. Fine with me. What about?
MOSES. I'll see you then.
CHAD. Yeah. Just come on up to the Tower when you're ready.
MOSES. Thank you.
DREW. What about?

>(**MOSES** *puts a finger against his lips.*
>
>*He exits.*
>
>*Silence.*
>
>**ANITA** *enters – stops.*)

DREW. Come on in. You'll get used to it in a minute.

>(**ANITA** *sits, lights a cigarette.*)

CHAD. Hi there.
ANITA. Hi.
DREW. Hello.
ANITA. Hi.

>(*Silence.*)

CHAD. I didn't know that about Moses.
DREW. About his wife?
CHAD. Yeah.
DREW. I thought everyone knew. It was in all the papers.

>(*Silence.*
>
>**ANITA** *covers her head with her arms.*)

DREW. Tough day? (*Pause.*)
ANITA. Yeah.

>(*Silence.*)
>
>…I just can't get it straight today. First I did it by numbers. And that was wrong. Then I did it by assignment. And that was wrong. Then I did it by names. And that

was wrong, too. I just can't get anything right today...I should've stayed home. Called in sick or something...I just wanna go home. I never should've gotten out of bed today.

CHAD. What department you in?

ANITA. Transportation.

CHAD. Diane, huh?

ANITA. God, yes.

DREW. Do I know her?

CHAD. Diane's the Transportation Facilitator.

DREW. Ah. *(Pause.)*

CHAD. What's she bitching about today?

ANITA. You really wanna know?

CHAD. Yeah.

ANITA. It's all so...Do you know her?

CHAD. I've met her, but I don't know her. *(Pause.)*

ANITA. If you really want to know, I'll tell you. But you've got to understand that I'm not saying anything about her, okay? I'm not criticizing her personal life, I'm just pointing out how her personal life affects things in Transport.

DREW. Gotcha. *(Pause.)*

ANITA. Diane's got this thing for gay guys. As employees. She loves 'em. If you're gay, you can do no wrong. You're not a threat. I mean, you know what Diane looks like, right? She's not exactly, uhhh...I don't know – name a movie star...The point is, a straight woman, a relatively good-looking straight woman, doesn't have a chance. *(Pause.)* Last Friday, I was showing some of the people in Transport a picture of my son. And everyone's oohing and ahhing over it, because he's really cute if I do say so myself. And I do...And Diane – Diane sees us all looking at it and she comes over and she's like, 'What's the occasion, folks?' And I show her the photograph – big mistake – and she's like, 'Oh! He's so...cute!' You know, like how could he be my son if he's so cute. What she's really saying is, 'You fucking breeder. You fucking heterosexual.' Totally sweet on the surface but totally dismissive underneath. So that's the background…Now this morning I just couldn't get the tallies right. Like I said, I tried it by names, numbers, assignments, everything, and it wouldn't add up. And I know it's important, and I know the trucks are waiting, and I know there's a very limited amount of time in which to get the job done. I understand that. And I did finally get it right and everything's okay. But then Diane calls me over to her cubicle and says she wants to have a little talk with me. I say sure and I go over. And we sit down and she's asking me if anything's wrong, am I feeling all right, am I having any problems…And I say no, which is true. Everything's fine. Pretty much. No major problems. And then she says well, she couldn't help but wonder because I seem to be having trouble lately with getting my work done accurately and on time. Which is so not true! I mean, you know how many people we process every day? It's not unusual to occasionally get – not confused, but temporarily lost…Overwhelmed. Plus, we're short on staff because of the hiring freeze. We're all working really hard trying to get everything done…And then she goes, 'I need to be able to depend on you, Anita. If I can't depend on you I may have to reassign you.' Jesus!…None of what she says is true, but that doesn't matter. I have no say in this at all. She's in charge, and if she wants me out of there she can do it like –

(She snaps her fingers.)

– that. And then I'm screwed. It's on my record, and don't even talk about the pay cut…And none of it has anything to do with my work. It's all because I'm a fucking heterosexual shit-bag breeder. *(Pause.)* I don't have anything against her. I just want to get the job done and make a living. I mean, look at me – I know a little something about discrimination.

(Silence.)

(She grinds out her cigarette, rises.)

I should get back.

(She crosses to the door.)

Thanks for listening, you guys.

DREW. Not a problem.

ANITA. Don't say anything about this to anyone, okay? I don't want to get in any more trouble...Have a good day.

CHAD. You, too.

(She exits.

Silence.)

DREW. Anita, huh?

CHAD. Anita. *(Pause.)*

DREW. Yummy.

(Silence.

DREW *grinds out his cigarette, rises.)*

All right. Let's get messy.

*(***CHAD** *grinds out his cigarette, rises.*

They exit.

Lights fade.)

3.

(Clock: 12:46.
Lights up.
TERRY *smokes, drinks coffee, reads the paper.*
TAMMIE *smokes, drinks coffee, leafs through a travel magazine.*
Silence.)

TERRY. …See the paper?

TAMMIE. …Somethin' in it?

TERRY. Kid collected a buncha old firecrackers. Tore 'em open and made a gun-powder pie. Dropped a match in it. Blam. Upper-lip pie. Blew half his face off.

TAMMIE. Oh, for Pete's sake…

TERRY. Then there's the thing about that guy. That movie star. What's his name. Old guy. *(Pause.)*

TAMMIE. Paul Newman?

TERRY. Wasn't Paul Newman. *(Pause.)*

TAMMIE. Clint the Squint?

TERRY. Wasn't him, either. It's in that pile somewhere. I don't remember his name.

(Silence.)

TAMMIE. What'd he do?

TERRY. Died.

(Silence.

TAMMIE *flips through her magazine.)*

Ooh. That looks nice…I'd like to go there.

TERRY. Where?

TAMMIE. Italy. *(Pause.)* I'm going to Cancun next month.

TERRY. That's cool. *(Pause.)*

TAMMIE. I never been out of the country. I hope I don't get drunk and screw some Mexican.

(Silence.)

TERRY. Expensive?

TAMMIE. …Hmmm?

TERRY. The trip?

TAMMIE. No. I got a good deal on it.

TERRY. That's good.

TAMMIE. Otherwise I couldn't go. You know?

(ESTELLE enters, sits, lights a cigarette.

Silence.)

TERRY. …How come if the economy's so good, my finances suck shit?

TAMMIE. Haven't you heard? We're in an upswing.

TERRY. Sure we are – if you believe them lyin' bitches in the White House, sure.

TAMMIE. I believe 'em.

TERRY. Believe your paycheck, what I say. *(Pause.)* Smoke and mirrors, man. That's all it is. Smoke and mirrors.

(Silence.

ESTELLE *take out a notebook, writes.)*

TERRY. Tell me again – why'd you quit dental school after two weeks?

TAMMIE. 'Cause it sucked.

TERRY. Then why'd you go?

TAMMIE. 'Cause I didn't know how bad it sucked.

(Silence.)

I went to hair school, though…And that I did all right at. Got the degree and everything. But I never practiced. Never worked in a salon. *(Pause.)*

TERRY. Why's that?

TAMMIE. I wasn't wearin' glasses then, and the chemicals were screwin' up my eyes. But I can do it. Cut hair, style it. Permanents. The whole thing. The whole ball of wax.

TERRY. …I used to have hair down to my ass.

TAMMIE. Me, too.

(Silence.)

My husband was a stylist. That's how we met. We were both in hair school together…Andrew. Andrew Wagner. He's Andrea Wagner, now, but then…

TERRY. Wait a minute…

TAMMIE. He got tired of tucking it up so he had it chopped off.

TERRY. Damn.

TAMMIE. Went to Sweden and everything.

TERRY. Damn!

TAMMIE. Hormones and everything. *(Pause.)* I don't see him much anymore. Moved to Denver with a guy named Duane. Even when he was still in town, our circles didn't exactly cross.

(Silence.)

I wouldn't be workin' this job if he paid me what he owed me.

(Silence.)

TERRY. He don't help you out at all?

TAMMIE. Every once in a while, yeah. But I can buy my own bras, thank you very much.

(Silence.

MOSES *at the door.)*

MOSES. Tammie, can you check 'S' Wing for me? I thought I'd take lunch now…If you're through.

TAMMIE. Sure.

MOSES. There's no rush. Finish your smoke. *(P.)* A bear goes into a bar. Says to the bartender, 'I'd like a gin…' *(Pause.)* '…and tonic.' Bartender says, 'Why the big pause?' Bear says, 'I don't know. My father had 'em, too.'

(He laughs.)

TAMMIE. …That's funny.

MOSES. Mona sent me that…I've got the keys, so just come to the cafeteria when you're done.

TAMMIE. Great.

*(****MOSES**** exits.*

Silence.)

TAMMIE. I tried those things. *(Pause.)*

TERRY. What?

TAMMIE. Those muffin things.

TERRY. You did, huh?

TAMMIE. Oh. Yeah. Yeah, I did. Sure.

(Silence.)

TERRY. Good?

TAMMIE. Pretty good…Different. I don't know if I'd try 'em again, but…Yeah, they were okay…What I really like's that chocolate pudding they had. You remember that? Now that was good. You could tell the whipped cream wasn't just out of a can…Someone took some time with that.

(Silence.)

I could eat that out of a tub.

(Silence.)

Did you have the tacos?

TERRY. I wouldn't eat here if they paid me. *(Pause.)*

TAMMIE. What do you do for lunch?

TERRY. Bring my own. Keep it in the fridge. Nuke it up.

(Silence.)

TAMMIE. Save a lot of money that way?

TERRY. Some.

(Silence.)

How were the tacos?

TAMMIE. That's what I keep askin' myself. *(Pause.)* Good, I guess, but…Somethin' about 'em just…I don't know. Somethin'…off. *(Pause.)* I don't know. *(Pause.)* The muffin thing was okay. I know that.

(Silence.

High-pitched electronic chirp.

TAMMIE *unclips her walkie-talkie from her waistband.)*

Yeah. *(Pause.)* I'm on my way.

(She clips the walkie-talkie back on her waistband, rises.)

All right…

TERRY. Doesn't let up, does he?

TAMMIE. He does not.

(She grinds out her cigarette.

She holds out the magazine to **TERRY.***)*

You wanna look at this?

TERRY. I don't mind.

(She gives **TERRY** *the magazine, crosses to the door.)*

Forgot your lighter.

TAMMIE. Shit.

(She crosses back, picks up her lighter, crosses to the door.)

Thank you.

TERRY. Not a problem.

*(***TAMMIE** *exits.*

Silence.)

TERRY. Hormones and everything…Damn.

(He opens the magazine.

Silence.

CHAD *– in a fresh labcoat – enters.)*

CHAD. Yo, Terry.

TERRY. Yo, Chad.

CHAD. Yo, Estelle.

*(***CHAD** *sits, lights a cigarette.*

ESTELLE *opens her purse, digs around in it.*

Silence.)

TERRY. How's everything in the Tower?

CHAD. It's goin' really well. We're gettin' a lot done…What you lookin' at?

TERRY. Italy.

*(**ESTELLE** takes a spray can of air freshener out of her bag.)*

CHAD. You thinkin' of goin'?

TERRY. I'm thinkin', but I ain't goin'.

CHAD. Ya never know. Now we got troops there…

TERRY. That's what they tell me.

*(**ESTELLE** rises, walks about the room spraying air freshener.)*

TERRY. Estelle, calm that shit down, okay?

CHAD. I'm used to it. It's all right.

TERRY. We gotta breath that shit, Estelle!

*(**ESTELLE** returns to her chair, sits, puts the air freshener away.*

Silence.)

CHAD. It clings to ya. What can I say? *(Pause.)* Mind if I take a look at that?

TERRY. Go ahead.

*(He tosses the magazine to **CHAD**.*

He pages through it.

Silence.)

…You have the tacos?

TERRY. No. *(Pause.)*

CHAD. Good.

TERRY. Yeah?

CHAD. Real good.

(Silence.

CHAD *flips through the magazine.)*

There's Rome…Italy's great. But I really love Japan.

What can I say? I'm an orientalist.

TERRY. No shit.

CHAD. In fact, I'm currently dating a very lovely young Japanese woman. Toriashi. She's somethin' else. Incredibly vigorous. Highly sexual. Saturday night we got a little drunk and you wouldn't believe the – well, first you gotta know that Tori's got a twin sister and –

(*DREW – in a fresh labcoat – opens the door.*)

DREW. Free cupcakes in the cafeteria!

CHAD. Fuck.

(*DREW closes the door.*

CHAD rises.)

You want a cupcake, Terry?

TERRY. That'd be all right.

CHAD. Cupcake comin' up.

(*He exits.*)

TERRY. You wanna get me some more coffee, too?

(*But the door is closed.*)

Shit.

(*Silence.*

ANITA *– carrying two cupcakes with red-white-and-blue frosting and a small American flag stuck in the center – enters.*

She sits, lights a cigarette.)

ANITA. Free cupcakes, Estelle. (*Pause.*)

(*Silence.*

She rises, places one of her cupcakes on **ESTELLE**'s *table.*

She picks up the travel magazine.)

Anyone reading this?

(*Silence.*

She returns with the magazine to her table.

She flips through its pages, smokes and eats.

Silence.

DREW – *with a red-white-and-blue cupcake and a cup of coffee – enters.*

He sits, lights a cigarette.

He smokes and eats.

Silence.)

DREW. God, those were some good tacos, huh?

(*Silence.*)

Did you have the tacos?

ANITA. I had the Chicken A La King.

DREW. How was it?

ANITA. Good. (*Pause.*) The biscuits were awful.

(*Silence.*)

TERRY. Lumpy?

ANITA. Dry…Too flaky…Not good.

(*Silence.*)

DREW. Anyone see *American Justice* last night?

TERRY. I was gonna watch it, but I fell asleep. How many people they kill?

DREW. Six.

TERRY. I heard seven on the radio comin' in.

DREW. Six…Well, seven if you count the Arab and the retard.

TERRY. …You tape it?

(**CHAD** – *with two red-white-and blue cupcakes and a cup of coffee – enters.*

He places a cupcake on **TERRY**'s *table.*)

CHAD. There ya go, brother-man.

TERRY. Thank you.

(**CHAD** *sits, lights a cigarette.*

He smokes and eats.

Silence.)

ANITA. ...Ireland looks nice.

CHAD. I been there.

ANITA. Is it really that green?

CHAD. Let me see.

(He rises, crosses to ANITA, looks at the magazine.)

CHAD. Yeah. *(Pause.)*

(CHAD returns to his table.

Silence.)

TERRY. You know the show I like?

DREW. Which one?

TERRY. ...Shit. Now I can't think of the name of it. *(Pause.)* *Secret* somethin'.

(Silence.

ANITA *puts the magazine down.)*

ANITA. I never go anywhere.

(Silence.)

TERRY. *Dirty Secrets.*

DREW. That's a good show.

TERRY. That's my favorite. Titties and *everything*.

(Silence.)

'Scuse me, ladies.

(Silence.

MOSES – *napkin tucked into collar, can of soda in hand* – *at the door.)*

MOSES. After lunch okay with you guys?

CHAD. Sure.

DREW. One-thirty? Something like that?

MOSES. See ya then.

(He starts to exit.)

DREW. Moses.

(MOSES stops.)

How about those tacos?

MOSES. They were good.

DREW. They were really good.

CHAD. Just like bein' in Mexico.

DREW. But no Mexicans.

MOSES. The tacos were good. Chips, too.

ANITA. The salsa they use is good.

CHAD. They never have guacamole, though.

MOSES. I noticed that.

DREW. One-thirty or so, come on up.

(MOSES exits.

Silence.)

TERRY. You guys see the paper? They found that girl.

(Silence.)

DREW. Anita?…It's Anita, right?

ANITA. Right.

DREW. Any better?

ANITA. …No. *(Pause.)* You-know-who's asked me to come talk with her and Richard.

DREW. Is that bad?

ANITA. Well…It's not good.

DREW. Jeez. *(Pause.)* Do I know Richard?

CHAD. He's the Transport Supervisor. Tall guy? Mustache?… Glasses?…Mole?…No?

DREW. Maybe if I saw him.

TERRY. You don't wanna see him. Stringy motherfucker.

ANITA. You really don't. Believe me. *(Pause.)* Anyway…

(Silence.)

DREW. Hope it goes okay.

ANITA. Thanks.

(Silence.)

CHAD. You hear the one about the bear? A bear goes into a bar –

ANITA. – 'Why the big pause?'

CHAD. You heard it, huh?…Okay. Two nuns go into a sex shop to get a dildo, and the first –

DREW. Hey, man.

CHAD. What?

DREW. Later. *(Pause.)*

CHAD. If it's okay to send it to people, it's gotta be okay to tell it.

DREW. Later.

(Silence.)

ANITA. I won't say I'm not worried. 'Cause I am. But things usually turn out better than you think they will. Usually.

(Silence.)

At least when it happens, you don't have to wonder anymore what's it gonna be like. *(Pause.)* You *know*.

(Silence.

TERRY *grinds out his cigarette, tosses the cupcake wrapper and flag in the trashbin.)*

DREW. Hey. You're not supposed to throw that away.

TERRY. …What?

DREW. That's a flag, dude. You're supposed to wear it. Put it in your lapel or something. Show some respect, you know?

(Silence.

TERRY *retrieves the flag from the trash.)*

TERRY. I'm supposed to wear this?

DREW. You don't have to, but you don't just throw it away.

CHAD. He's right.

(Silence.)

TERRY. This is a flag?

(Silence.)

(He turns to **ANITA**.*)*

Anita – this a flag?

ANITA. Yeah…I guess.

(Silence.)

TERRY. Nothin' but flags in here, huh?

(Silence.)

CHAD. Damn! Where's yo' nappy head at, brother-man? Chill!

(Silence.)

TERRY. Sorry, y'all. I thought it was just a piece of paper on a toothpick. But y'all say it's a flag, so…Shit. Huh… My mistake. So if I do this –

(He takes out his lighter, sets the little flag on fire.)

– you tellin' me I committed a crime?…I mean, is that a crime? I'm serious here. Is that a crime? *(Pause.)*

DREW. Not yet. *(Pause.)*

TERRY. Let me get this straight.

(He crosses to a table, draws on a section of newspaper.

He tears off the section, holds up his drawing: a crude flag.)

This a flag, too? *(Pause.)*

CHAD. No.

TERRY. Why not? 'Cause it ain't in color?

(Silence.)

So this ain't a flag, but that little piece of paper on a toothpick is.

(Silence.)

So it's okay with y'all if I burn this.

(He sets the piece of newspaper on fire…drops it into the trashbin.

Silence.)

ANITA. What are you gettin' at, Terry?

TERRY. I'm just tryin' to figure out what's a flag and what's not. We got a problem here, I wanna solve it.

DREW. Look, I was only making the point –

TERRY. No, man. No. No. I heard what you said. I think it's pretty clear. I think you've expressed yourself. And that's what's got me curious 'bout this here. 'Cause I was workin' on the assumption that all a flag is is a, a… representation of a mode of life, know what'm sayin'? Of a mode of behavior. I didn't know it was the thing itself. 'Cause if that's the case I just fucked up big-time. I'm not free anymore. Damn! Sorry, y'all!

DREW. Terry, you're makin' way too much outta this.

TERRY. I don't think so. I don't think so…Drew. We talkin' 'bout principles here, right? Well, I'm interested in principles.

DREW. Look – you threw the fuckin' thing away. Fine. It's not a flag. Fine. So just shut the fuck up and let it go, okay? Fuckin' let it go.

(*Silence.*)

ANITA. Terry?…Just let it go.

(*Silence.*

TERRY *places the fingertips of one hand on his forehead.*

Silence.

He lowers his hand.)

There. I just burned a flag in my mind. Is that a crime?

DREW. For fuck's sake, Terry.

(*Silence.*

TERRY *crosses to a table, draws on a section of newspaper.*

He holds up the section of newspaper: a stick figure and the words 'The President of the United States'.)

TERRY. Now if I burn this, am I –

(Drew rises.)

Silence.)

DREW. That's not funny, Terry. That's not funny at all. And I want you to know how deeply offensive I find your actions. In fact, I'm appalled. I know you're making a point. I get your point. I don't agree with it, but I get it and I understand it. But now you've crossed the line. And there will be repercussions. Mark my words. All I can say is, I hope there's a breadline in your neighborhood – 'Cause you're gonna be on it. If they don't throw your ass in jail first.

(He crosses to the door.)

You black bastard.

(He exits.

Silence.

CHAD *rises.*

He puts his tiny flag in his lapel.

He exits.

Silence.)

ANITA. Oh, Terry…

(Silence.)

TERRY. All my life, it's been one motherfucker like that after another…

(Silence.

TERRY *exits.)*

ANITA. Terry!

(Pause. **TERRY** *enters.)*

ANITA. …Be careful. *(Pause.)*

TERRY. You and me both.

(He exits.

Silence.

ESTELLE *reaches into her purse, takes out a notebook and pen, writes.*

Silence.

She puts the notebook and pen back into her purse.

She rises, picks up her cupcake, exits.

Silence.)

ANITA. Oh, Terry…

(She lights a cigarette.

Silence.

She checks the clock, checks her wristwatch.

She takes a paperback out of her purse.

She opens the paperback.

She sets it down.

She smokes.

Silence.

MOSES *at door.)*

MOSES. Anita? Mind if we come in?

ANITA. …No. No, not all. 'Course not.

MOSES. Thank you.

*(**MOSES** – followed by **TAMMIE** – enters.*

They sit, light cigarettes, smoke.)

Sorry to interrupt. Have you got a minute? Or two?

ANITA. …Of course, sure.

MOSES. Thank you…What are you reading?

ANITA. This? Oh. It's a…It's a mystery. A detective story. Sort of a detective story.

MOSES. What's it about? What's the plot?

ANITA. Well…Ummm…Well, it's…It's about a detective who goes home because his father is dying.

MOSES. Ah. *(Pause.)*

ANITA. And, uh…At the hospital he meets up with this woman who used to be the detective's girlfriend. You know, a long time ago. And what happens is, Claire – that's the name of the girlfriend, the former girlfriend – Claire's father is also in the hospital....He's got Alzheimer's.

MOSES. The detective or the father?

ANITA. The father. Claire's father. *(Pause.)*

MOSES. Go on.

ANITA. And, then, uh...I'm not very far along in it, really, but...It's something like Alzheimer's. Something like that. His memory's affected, though. He talks and it doesn't make sense. So...the – Claire tells the detective that something her father said has to do with her mother's death. Which everyone believed was an accident, but from things the old man's been saying might actually be murder. And maybe he's the one who did it. Her father. So she asks the detective to look into the case. Well, it's not a case, but the circumstances surrounding her mother's death 20...25 years ago.

MOSES. Does he find out what really happened?

ANITA. I'm not that far along yet. I'll bet he does. I mean, I'm sure he does. *(Pause.)*

MOSES. You could say he's investigating the past.

ANITA. Yeah.

MOSES. That's dangerous. *(Pause.)*

ANITA. I guess so, yeah. It could be. Sure. *(Pause.)*

(She rises.)

I should go. I've gotta get ready for a meeting.

MOSES. You've got plenty of time. They know you're with us. *(Pause.)* Have another smoke.

(Pause. **ANITA** *sits, lights a cigarette.)*

You read a lot, Anita? You like to read?

ANITA. I guess so. Yeah. Yes.

MOSES. All kinds of stuff, or just mysteries?

ANITA. All kinds of stuff.

*(***MOSES*** takes a folded sheet of paper from an inside*

breastpocket.)

MOSES. You ever read this?

ANITA. …What is it?

MOSES. Something that's been floating around the building.

(He holds it out to ANITA.)

Take a look at it.

ANITA. Is this the thing about the two nuns and the dildo?

MOSES. No. I'm sad to say it's not. *(Pause.)* Take it.

(ANITA takes the paper, unfolds it, reads.)

…You ever read that? Ever see it before?

(ANITA re-folds the paper, sets it down. Pause.)

ANITA. No. I haven't.

MOSES. You've never seen it and you've never read it. 'Till now.

ANITA. That's right.

MOSES. Do you know anyone who has? *(Pause.)*

ANITA. No.

MOSES. You're sure?

ANITA. Yes.

MOSES. Do you know who might have written it? *(Pause.)*

ANITA. No.

MOSES. No idea?

ANITA. No. *(Pause.)*

MOSES. Well, I was hoping someone would. It'd make our job that much easier. I don't take it seriously, you understand. After all, we're all entitled to our own opinions. Am I right?

(ANITA nods.)

But Administration feels – and I tend to agree with them on this – that in times like these, a thing like this is…worrisome. A sign of – how'd they put it?…A sign of discontent in an otherwise happy, productive and unified…

(He turns to **TAMMIE**.*)*

A unified what?

TAMMIE. …Endeavor.

MOSES. Endeavor. There you have it. *(Pause.)* And it's not as if they're really worried. I mean, when all is said and done, who cares what people think? They're going to do what they're going to do. But they asked me – and Tammie – to check around and see what we could find out. And that's why we're sitting here now. Smoking like fiends and shooting the breeze.

(He picks up the sheet of paper, holds it out to **ANITA**.*)*

Would you read it to me?

(Silence.)

Tammie, would you read this to me, please?

*(***TAMMIE** *unfolds the paper, reads.)*

TAMMIE. 'My Country, 'Tis Of Thee.'

(She looks at **MOSES**.*)*

MOSES. Go on. *(Pause.)*

TAMMIE. 'A country held hostage by a fanatical dictator…A country that possesses weapons of mass destruction…A country that flouts domestic and international law with impunity…A country mad enough to even contemplate the use of nuclear weapons…A country like this must be held accountable for its actions. The reckless, criminal, amoral behavior of a country like that must be stopped in its tracks.' *(Pause.)* 'My country, 'tis of thee I speak. The merest glance beneath the officially sanctioned news sources reveals without a doubt the real reasons for America's latest rush to war. The real reasons are breathtakingly simple, breathtakingly transparent no matter how cunningly disguised in the bunting of patriotic rhetoric: The United States' quest for Empire, its desire for world-wide hegemony over resources (oil, primarily) and people (who represent the markets that Capitalism demands to further impoverish the poor and make the rich richer).' *(Pause.)* 'In service of this quest, which is supported and rationalized by a worldview as Manichean and apocalyptic as that of the supposed "enemy," there are no depths to which the United States will not sink. Facts will be twisted, the historical record rewritten, fustian and bombast will be used to manipulate its wary, frightened citizens. The true destructiveness of war – the way it rips limbs from bodies, heads from torsos, the way men, women and children suffer when wells have no water that isn't contaminated, when depleted uranium wreaks havoc on bones and brains now and into perpetuity, when the gutters run with blood and sewage, when the entire infrastructure of a country's been destroyed – all this will be downplayed, ignored, forgotten. *(Pause.)* 'In service of this quest fake crises will be created, such as the im – imbro…'

MOSES. 'Imbroglio'.

TAMMIE. ' – imbroglio over "weapons of mass destruction," while real, ongoing crises such as the continued persecution of the Palestinian people by the state of Israel with economic and military assistance from the United States, will be downplayed, ignored, forgotten.' *(Pause.)* 'Forgotten, at least, by the ones responsible for the damage and chaos. Those who have no choice but to live in chaos cannot forget.' *(Pause.)* 'This is the challenge we face: How do we change a system that not only thrives on war – the preparations beforehand, the reparations after, the whole ugly process of demolishing and rebuilding that benefits only the demolitionists – but is itself the cause of war?' *(Pause.)* 'How do we change this?' *(Pause.)* 'How?' *(Pause.)* 'How?' *(Pause.)* 'How?'

(Silence.

TAMMIE *re-folds the piece of paper, holds it out to* **MOSES**.

MOSES *tucks it into an inside breast-pocket.*)

MOSES. Thank you, Tammie. *(Pause.)* Preaching to the converted, but still…You can see why Administration might be perturbed. What if someone took it seriously? *(Pause.)* That's all we wanted. If you hear anything, you'll let us know, won't you?

ANITA. Yes. Of course.

MOSES. All right, then.

(**ANITA** *rises, starts to go.*)

MOSES. Anita?

(She stops, turns.)

There's nothing wrong with telling the truth.

(Silence.)

If you know something, Anita, I really wish you'd tell me.

(Silence.)

We're pretty sure who it is, Anita. All we need is confirmation.

(Silence.)

I'd hate to think you were covering up for someone.

(Silence.)

ANITA. I don't know anything. Really.

(Silence.)

MOSES. I believe you, Anita. Because I want to believe you. *(Pause.)* Sorry to have kept you from your meeting.

(**ANITA** *starts to go.*)

I'm sorry – one more thing.

(**ANITA** *stops.*)

If you see Terry anywhere, would you tell him we'd like to see him? If he's still in the building.

(Silence.)

ANITA. I don't know anything, but…

(Silence.)

But you might ask Diane about the…

(Silence.

She starts to go.)

MOSES. Anita?

(She stops.)

Sometime you'll have to tell me the one about the two nuns and the dildo. I'll bet it's a hoot.

(Pause. She exits.

Silence.

Lights fade.)

4.

(Clock: 2:35
Lights up.
MOSES – *with a cup of coffee* – *sits and smokes.*
ANITA – *with file folders* – *in doorway.)*

ANITA. I'm going to the meeting now. Wish me luck.

(Silence.

MOSES *nods.)*

ANITA. Thanks.

(She exits.

TAMMIE – *with a cup of coffee* – *enters...stops.*

She crosses to one the tables, sits, lights a cigarette.

She takes a roll of antacid tablets out of her jacket pocket.

She eats one, takes a swig of coffee.

She eats another, takes another swig of coffee.

She eats a third, takes a third swig of coffee.

Silence.

MOSES *unclips his walkie-talkie, presses a button.*

High-pitched electronic chirp from **TAMMIE***'s walkie-talkie.*

TAMMIE *unclips her walkie-talkie.)*

TAMMIE. Yeah.

MOSES. Tammie, Moses here. Why aren't you at the front desk? Over.

(Silence.

TAMMIE *presses a button on her walkie-talkie.*

High-pitched electronic chirp from **MOSES'** *walkie-talkie.)*

MOSES. Yeah.

TAMMIE. Moses, Tammie here. I'm not at the front desk

'cause I'm not feelin' well.

Over.

(Silence.

MOSES *presses a button on his walkie-talkie.*

High-pitched electronic chirp from **TAMMIE***'s walkie-talkie.)*

TAMMIE. Yeah.

MOSES. What's wrong? Over.

(Silence.

TAMMIE *presses a button on her walkie-talkie.*

High-pitched electronic chirp from **MOSES***' walkie-talkie.)*

MOSES. Yeah.

TAMMIE. My stomach. Over.

(Silence.

MOSES *presses a button on his walkie-talkie.*

High-pitched electronic chirp from **TAMMIE***'s walkie-talkie.)*

TAMMIE. Yeah.

MOSES. Nausea, burning – what?

(Silence.)

You read me? Over.

TAMMIE *doubles over.*

Silence.

TAMMIE *presses a button on her walkie-talkie.*

High-pitched electronic chirp from **MOSES***' walkie-talkie.)*

MOSES. Yeah.

TAMMIE. I'm sorry – could you repeat the question? Over.

(Silence.

MOSES *presses a button on his walkie-talkie.*

High-pitched electronic chirp from **TAMMIE***'s walkie-talkie.)*

TAMMIE. Yeah.

MOSES. I said –

TAMMIE. Oh, shit.

(She rises, hurries out of the room.

MOSES *rises.)*

MOSES. Tammie – you okay? Tammie?

*(***CHAD** *– in blood-spattered labcoat, cup of coffee in hand – in doorway.*

He walks a few steps into the room, leans over and vomits.)

CHAD. Oh, shit...

(He slumps into a chair as **MOSES** *exits quickly.*

DREW *– in blood-spattered labcoat, cup of coffee in hand – enters.*

He sits, takes out his cigarettes and lighter – and vomits between his knees.)

DREW. Oh, shit...

*(***CHAD** *rises, hurries out of the room.*

TAMMIE *in doorway.*

DREW *rushes to the trashbin, sticks his head into it, retches.*

TAMMIE *cups her hands over her mouth and hurries out of the room.*

MOSES *– with paper towels – enters, stops, grabs his stomach, Exits.*

CHAD *enters – sits – rises quickly – heads for door – vomits – Exits.*

DREW *rises and hurries out of the room.*

CHAD *enters, sits, lights a cigarette, rests with head in hands.*

TERRY – *jacket, satchel – enters.*

He unclips his photo-I.D. badge.)

TERRY. No one at the desk to give this to, so…

(He tosses the photo-I.D. badge into the trash.)

Nice workin' with ya. *(Pause.)*

CHAD. You fucking – terrorist. *(Pause.)*

TERRY. You don't gotta worry about me. We ain't runnin' this show. We don't count. We're just the niggers who build the pyramid.

CHAD. Get the fuck outta here!

TERRY. You got it…Brother-man.

(He crosses to the emergency exit, opens it.

Blaring siren.

Flashing lights.

TERRY *walks through the emergency exit.*

MOSES *in doorway.)*

MOSES. Everybody out! Everybody out! – Go! Go! Go! Now! Go! Go!

(He runs off down the hall as **CHAD** *picks up his cigarette and leaves through the emergency exit.*

TAMMIE – *walkie-talkie in hand – enters at a clip, goes through the emergency exit.*

ESTELLE *walks calmly through the room, and through the emergency exit.*

DREW – *holding up his pants with one hand, sports page in the other – stumbles into the room and through the emergency exit.*

MOSES – *walkie-talkie in hand – enters the room and hurries out the emergency exit.*

Siren blares…

Lights flash…

Siren dies.

Lights return to normal.

Silence.

CHAD *enters through emergency exit, grinds out his cigarette, leaves through the door. Pause.*

ESTELLE *enters through the emergency exit, grinds out her cigarette, leaves through door. Pause.*

DREW *enters through emergency exit, grinds out his cigarette, leaves through door. Pause.*

MOSES *and* **TAMMIE** *enter through the emergency exit.*

They sit, light cigarettes.

MOSES *rises and exits, followed by* **TAMMIE**.

Silence.

MOSES *enters with mop and bucket, begins cleaning the floor.*

Silence.

TAMMIE *enters with a sponge and a bucket of water, begins cleaning the tables and chairs.*

Silence.

TAMMIE *exits with bucket and sponge.*

MOSES *exits with mop and bucket.*

TAMMIE *enters, sits, smokes.*

MOSES *enters, sits, smokes.*)

TAMMIE. Last time I eat the tacos here…

(Lights fade.)

5.

(Clock: 4:53

Lights up.

ESTELLE – *coat and bag on the chair beside her – smokes, pages through her notebook. P.*

CHAD *and* **DREW** – *coats, hats, satchels – in doorway.*

CHAD *taps on the door.)*

DREW. Night, Estelle.

CHAD. Don't stay up too late rockin' and rollin'.

DREW. Hell of a day, huh?

(Silence.

They exit.)

CHAD. *(OFF)* So Tori's sister – her twin sister, you gotta remember that – Saturday night they switch places with each other. So I'm pumpin' away…

(Silence.)

*(***TAMMIE** – *coat, shoulder bag – in doorway.*

She looks around the room.)

TAMMIE. …There it is.

(She crosses to a table, picks up a lighter.)

Knew I left it somewhere…Have a good night, Estelle.

*(***ANITA** – *coat, purse, cardboard box of office supplies – enters.)*

ANITA. Hi, Tammie.

TAMMIE. Hey, 'Nita. Done for the day?

ANITA. You could say that, yeah. *(Pause.)* I'm being transferred. *(Pause.)* 'Transferred' is what they call it. 'Fired' is what they mean.

TAMMIE. You're kiddin' me.

ANITA. Nope.

TAMMIE. That's not right!

ANITA. A mistake's a mistake. And mistakes were made. So…

(**TAMMIE** *crosses to* **ANITA**, *hugs her.*)

TAMMIE. You're a sweet little thing, you know that? You're gonna do just fine wherever you go next. I can tell that about you.

ANITA. You're sweet, too, Tammie. We're all gonna be okay. I know we are.

(**MOSES** – *coat, shoulder bag* – *enters.*)

MOSES. You still want a ride to the bus stop?

TAMMIE. Yeah.

MOSES. Well, come on, then.

TAMMIE. I'm just sayin' goodbye to Anita. She's bein' transferred.

MOSES. …I heard. I'm sorry to hear that.

ANITA. Oh, you know – onward and upward, right?

(Silence.)

MOSES. You heard about Terry?

ANITA. What?

MOSES. Terry is no longer – a part of our team. There'll be an official…thing about it tomorrow. Morale and all that. Extraordinary times call for extraordinary measures and all that…stuff. *(Pause.)*

ANITA. Was he the one? *(Pause.)*

MOSES. One who what?

ANITA. Sent that thing around? – That letter?

(Silence.

TAMMIE *crosses to a chair, sits, lights a cigarette.)*

MOSES. No, actually. He wasn't. I shouldn't be tellin' you this as you're being…transferred, but…Administration tracked his e-mail here and at his home, and he didn't download it or print it up. So it's gotta be someone else. *(Pause.)* He could have, though. Might have in the future. He fits the profile perfectly. *(Pause.)* So there it is. Who knows?

ANITA. Who knows.

MOSES. We'll find out, though…Won't we, Estelle? Sooner or later we'll get him. *(Pause.)* Or her. Whichever it is. *(Pause.)* Jesus, what a day. I'm beat to my socks.

TAMMIE. I'm ready to go whenever you are. *(Pause.)*

MOSES. I like the job, don't get me wrong. I like working, period. It gives a sense of shape and purpose to your life, you know?

ANITA. …Yeah.

MOSES. Otherwise it's all just…just a…

(Silence.)

Just…nothin'.

(Silence.)

Come on, Tam.

He exits.

TAMMIE *grinds out her cigarette, crosses to* **ANITA***, hugs her again.)*

TAMMIE. Be good, okay?

ANITA. I will.

MOSES. *(OFF)* Tammie!

TAMMIE. Gotta run. Take care now!

(She hurries out the door.)

ANITA. Bye!

(Silence.

ANITA *moves a few steps toward* **ESTELLE***.)*

Estelle?

*(***ESTELLE** *looks up.)*

Pardon me for interrupting. But I just wanted to…We don't really know each other very well – at all, really – but I just want to wish you the best, too. I hope – I hope you have a happy life. *(Pause.)*

*(***ESTELL** *returns to her notebook.*

Pause. **ANITA** *slowly starts to exit.)*

ESTELLE. ...Thank you.

(**ANITA** *stops, turns.*)

That's very kind of you. I, too, wish you all the best.

(She and **ANITA** *look at each other.*

Silence.

ESTELLE *grinds out her cigarette.*

She flips through her notebook...stops...separates two pages from the others...tears the pages from her notebook.

She holds them out to Anita.

Pause. Anita sets the cardboard box down on one of the tables, crosses to **ESTELLE**, *takes the pages.*

Never say we are not merciful.

(Pause. She closes the notebook, places pen and notebook in her purse. She rises, picks up her purse and coat.)

...I wouldn't linger. The gates are closing.

(She exits.

Silence.

ANITA *looks through the pages.*

She slowly folds the pages, puts them in her purse.

She exits.

Silence.

ANITA *returns.*

She crosses to the table, picks up the cardboard box.

She crosses to the door.

She turns the handle.

The door won't open.

She shifts the box to the other arm, tries again.

The door won't open.

She sets the box down.

She tries the door again.

The door won't open.

She taps on the door.)

Hello. Anyone out there?…Hello? Can somebody help me?

(Silence.)

Moses?…Anyone there?…Tammie?…Hello, I'm in here! Hello!

(She pounds on the door.)

I need some – assistance here! Hello!

(Silence.)

Hello!

(She pounds harder.)

Hello! Hello!… HEYYYY!

(Silence.)

HEY! HELLO! HELP ME!

(She pounds harder still.)

HEY! SOMEBODY! HELP ME HERE!

(Silence.

The overhead lights snap off.

Dim light in the room.

She grabs the door handle and rattles it furiously.)

HELP ME!

(Silence.)

HELP ME!

(Silence.)

HELP ME! HELLO! HELP! HELP ME! HELP ME! HELLLPPP!

(Silence.)

HELLLLLLLLLLLPPP!

(Silence.)

HELLLLLLLLLLLLLLLLPPPPPPP!

(Silence.)

HELLLLLLLLLLLLLLLLLLLLLLLPPPPPP!

(She pounds frantically on the door.)

HELLLLLLLLLLLLLLLLLLLLLLLLLLPPPPPP!

(She flails wildly at the door with her fists and feet and body)

AAAAGGGGGHHHHH!
AAAAAAAAAAAGGGGGGGHHHHHHHH!
AAAAAAAAAAAAAAAAAGGGGGGGGGGGGGGHH-
HHHHHHHHHHHHHH!

(Silence.

She turns, exhausted, breathing heavily, and rests with her back against the door.

She slowly slides to the floor.

She sits there.

She rises, crosses to the emergency exit, pushes the release bar.

The emergency exit won't open.

She pushes the release bar again.

The emergency exit won't open.

She steps back, throws herself against the emergency exit.

Nothing.

She throws herself against it again.

…And again.

…And again.

…And again.

…And again.

Nothing.

She rests her forehead against the emergency exit.)

Oh God, oh God, oh God, oh God…

(She walks slowly to the middle of the room.

She stands there.

She walks back to the table.

She slumps into a chair.

She sits there.

She lights a cigarette, smokes.

She rises, crosses to the cardboard box.

She takes out a small stuffed dog wearing a top hat and a ribbon around its neck.

She crosses back to her table.

She places the dog in the chair opposite her.

She sits.

She smokes.

Dim light fades.

Darkness.)

PROPS

SCENE 1:

MOSES: Walkie-talkie.
ANITA: Cigarettes, lighter, cup of coffee, small photograph.
TERRY: Cigarettes, lighter, cup of coffee, newspaper.
TAMMIE: Cigarettes, lighter, cup of coffee.

SCENE 2:

ESTELLE: Cigarettes, lighter, purse, pen and notebook.
CHAD: Cigarettes, lighter, cup of coffee.
DREW: Cigarettes, lighter, cup of coffee.

SCENE 3:

TERRY: Cigarettes, lighter, newspaper, black Sharpie pen.
TAMMIE: Cigarettes, lighter, travel magazine, walkie-talkie.
ESTELLE: Cigarettes, lighter, pen, notebook, purse, can of air freshener.
CHAD: Cigarettes, lighter, 2 cupcakes as described in play.
DREW: Cigarettes, lighter, cupcake as described in play.
ANITA: Cigarettes, lighter, 2 cupcakes as described in play, purse, paperback book.
MOSES: Can of soda, paper napkin.

SCENE 4:

MOSES: Cup of coffee, walkie-talkie, paper towels, mop and bucket.
ANITA: File folders.
TAMMIE: Roll of antacid tablets, walkie-talkie, coffee, sponge, bucket of water.
CHAD: Cigarettes, lighter, cup of coffee.
DREW: Cigarettes, lighter, cup of coffee, sports section of a newspaper.
TERRY: Photo I.D. badge.

SCENE 5:

ESTELLE: Purse, cigarettes, lighter, pen, notebook.

CHAD: Satchel.
DREW: Satchel.
TAMMIE: Shoulder bag, cigarettes, lighter.
ANITA: Purse, cigarettes, lighter, cardboard box with office supplies and stuffed dog as described in play.
MOSES: Shoulder bag, cigarettes, lighter.

COSTUMES

SCENE 1:

MOSES: Black suit, tie, sky-blue shirt, black oxfords.
ANITA: Slacks, blouse, jacket.
TERRY: Pants, shirt, back support belt (for heavy lifting–the kind worn by movers, for example).
TAMMIE: Black suit, tie, sky-blue shirt, black oxfords.

SCENE 2:

ESTELLE: Conservative dress or pantsuit.
CHAD: Blood-spattered lab coat over dark suit and tie.
DREW: Blood-spattered lab coat over dark suit and tie.

SCENE 3:

CHAD: Clean lab coat.
DREW: Clean lab coat.

SCENE 4:

CHAD: Blood-spattered lab coat.
DREW: Blood-spattered lab coat.

SCENE 5:

ESTELLE: Coat.
CHAD: Coat, hat.
DREW: Coat, hat.
TAMMIE: Coat.
ANITA: Coat.
MOSES: Coat.

From the Reviews of
SMOKE AND MIRRORS...

"Joseph Goodrich's dystopian office fantasy captures the glacial, disjointed rhythm of workplace conversations in an employee smoking lounge; it's a kind of nine-to-five prison yard, in which we see the grotesque and the ordinary conjoined."
- *The New Yorker*

"Everyone's out to get you in *Smoke and Mirrors*, a workplace comedy so dark it's completely believable...The oblique way in which *Smoke and Mirrors* gets at issues larger than the tedium of office work, the petit pettiness of paper shuffling, mimics the way the paranoia of national security has trickled down to the hoi polloi."
- *New Theatre Corps.*

"In *Smoke and Mirrors*, playwright Joseph Goodrich conjures up a wickedly amusing portrait of a stultifying but nerve-racking workplace."
- *Backstage.com*

"If Kafka scripted an episode of *The Office*, it might resemble Joseph Goodrich's bizarre and often intriguing *Smoke and Mirrors*, set in the smoking room of a nebulous American corporation."
- *Time Out New York*

"Goodrich has written a well-crafted, thought-provoking play that trusts the audience to fill in the blanks, yet gives them enough information to do so. He has wit and insight aplenty, and establishes himself as a playwright to keep an eye on."
- *nytheatre.com*

Also by
Joseph Goodrich...

Panic

Please visit our website **samuelfrench.com** for complete descriptions and licensing information

OTHER TITLES AVAILABLE FROM SAMUEL FRENCH

EURYDICE
Sarah Ruhl

Dramatic Comedy / 5m, 2f / Unit Set

In *Eurydice*, Sarah Ruhl reimagines the classic myth of Orpheus through the eyes of its heroine. Dying too young on her wedding day, Eurydice must journey to the underworld, where she reunites with her father and struggles to remember her lost love. With contemporary characters, ingenious plot twists, and breathtaking visual effects, the play is a fresh look at a timeless love story.

"RHAPSODICALLY BEAUTIFUL. A weird and wonderful new play - an inexpressibly moving theatrical fable about love, loss and the pleasures and pains of memory."
- The New York Times

"EXHILARATING!! A luminous retelling of the Orpheus myth, lush and limpid as a dream where both author and audience swim in the magical, sometimes menacing, and always thrilling flow of the unconscious."
- *The New Yorker*

"Exquisitely staged by Les Waters and an inventive design team… Ruhl's wild flights of imagination, some deeply affecting passages and beautiful imagery provide transporting pleasures. They conspire to create original, at times breathtaking, stage pictures."
- *Variety*

"Touching, inventive, invigoratingly compact and luminously liquid in its rhythms and design, *Eurydice* reframes the ancient myth of ill-fated love to focus not on the bereaved musician but on his dead bride – and on her struggle with love beyond the grave as both wife and daughter."
- *The San Francisco Chronicle*

SAMUELFRENCH.COM

OTHER TITLES AVAILABLE FROM SAMUEL FRENCH

EVIL DEAD: THE MUSICAL
Book & Lyrics By George Reinblatt
Music By Frank Cipolla/Christopher Bond/Melissa Morris/
George Reinblatt

Musical Comedy / 6m, 4f / Unit set

Based on Sam Raimi's 80s cult classic films, *Evil Dead* tells the tale of 5 college kids who travel to a cabin in the woods and accidentally unleash an evil force. And although it may sound like a horror, its not! The songs are hilariously campy and the show is bursting with more farce than a Monty Python skit. *Evil Dead: The Musical* unearths the old familiar story: boy and friends take a weekend getaway at abandoned cabin, boy expects to get lucky, boy unleashes ancient evil spirit, friends turn into Candarian Demons, boy fights until dawn to survive. As musical mayhem descends upon this sleepover in the woods, "camp" takes on a whole new meaning with uproarious numbers like "All the Men in my Life Keep Getting Killed by Candarian Demons," "Look Who's Evil Now" and "Do the Necronomicon."

Outer Critics Circle nomination for
Outstanding New Off-Broadway Musical

"The next Rocky Horror Show!"
- *New York Times*

"A ridiculous amount of fun."
- *Variety*

"Wickedly campy good time."
- *Associated Press*

SAMUELFRENCH.COM

www.ingramcontent.com/pod-product-compliance
Lightning Source LLC
Chambersburg PA
CBHW070650300426
44111CB00013B/2355